bush
PUBLISHING
& associates

Stop, *Listen* God Is Still Speaking Today

Dare to Listen, When God Wants to Speak

BY

BARBARA MYERS

Table of Contents

Acknowledgements

First of all, to the Holy Spirit who guided me through all these pages. To my husband Dr. Ray Myers for the much needed encouragement, his prayers and his love. I might add, "a pinch of patience."

To my nephew Lyle Smith who has tried for years to get me to write a book. He even bought me books on "How to" write a book.

Also Patty Poag. For her interest in my testimony and her encouragement, that I should pass it on. She convinced me that someone would benefit from my fellowship with God, and how He walked me through the loss of our son.

All credits of references in this book goes to the following:

Tony Ham, who gave us the Word from God and encouraged me to put my testimony into a book form.

My sisters, Betty Hein, Linda Green, Eunice Ulum, Donna Penland, and my niece Sherri Lawson. All inspired me in one way or another, and are in the book.

Lafonda and Eileen Damrom, whom I have loved and considered great friends for over forty years. God used them in my dreams.

Thank you all very much and God Bless You.

Foreword by Kenneth Isom

We've all gone through difficult times in our lives when we needed to hear from God. Not just the general instructions and guidelines of scripture, but personalized message from our Heavenly Father, a word that settles it, that affirms our place in His heart and gives us assurance that we are on track and are pleasing to Him.

Barbara, in her straightforward style, allows us to share those intimate moments when God has supernaturally shown up and spoken peace to an unsettled time. You will marvel at the many ways that God has used to reveal Himself.

In the process you will find yourself being more sensitive to the voice of God. He is not silent, but if we don't listen and remain quiet long enough to discern His voice, we might very well miss it. Absorb these powerful testimonies and then allow them to create a hunger in you for your own visitation,

Dr. Kenneth Isom, DVM
Board President, Teen Challenge of Oklahoma
Associate Pastor, The Bridge Assembly of God

Foreword

Does God still speak to his people today? Many Christians say an emphatic "Yes!" I once heard the late Dr. Adrian Rogers, a Baptist pastor, say, "God spoke to me the other day...no it wasn't an audible voice...it was much louder than that."

Barbara Myers has put together several stories of how God has spoken to her throughout her life. These messages, whether through vision, voices, or visitations, have all given her strength at times when she needed it most.

I've often tempered my own spiritual experiences of sensing the mysteriousness of God by saying something like, "I felt in my heart..." or "I sensed...." Barbara doesn't waste time tempering her words. She steps boldly forward and proclaims that God supernatural intervened at certain times in her life in visions or clearly stated words. She's not afraid of what people might say or think (as I must be). Her words are bold. Her stories are real. Her stories may be your stories too, especially if you've lost a child.

Read to be blessed. Read to be challenged. Examine your own faith in the light of your own experiences. To paraphrase Socrates, "An unexamined faith is not worth living."
—John Starnes
Recording Artist, Nashville, Tennessee

Introduction

Who am I? I am a seventy-five year old mother, grandmother and a great-grandmother, a home maker and a Pastor's wife, a sister to seven sisters, as well as a spirit filled child of God. I am a friend to those who let me and I love all with whom I come in contact. I say that one of the gifts God gave me is "a bucketful of love." Every time I pour out a cup of love He fills me back up. I had a Pastor's wife tell me once, "If I could have a friend, it would be you." I found out later (after becoming a pastor's wife) that it is an unwritten rule that a pastor's wife cannot have friends. I told them I would die if I could not have friends. I even had a lady come up to me in one church and ask, "Can I be your friend?" I had never been asked that question before, so I was a little taken aback. I mean, who am I that someone would ask such a question? I've always had a low self esteem and have never thought I was anyone special. But I am special. If I had nothing else going for me but that fact that Jesus loves me, I would be special. I am blessed abundantly.

My Sheep Know My Voice

In the Bible, Johns 10:4, Jesus mentions that His sheep know His voice. God has spoken to me several times in the past. I'm so thankful to I knew His voice. I am also thankful that I worked at knowing His voice. Especially since there are other voices that try to get our attention.

The incident I want to tell happened in Hartford, Connecticut, in nineteen ninety. My thirty year old son, Tim was on drugs and was out of control, I was ready to ask him to leave our home. My husband and I were on staff in a large Assembly of God church in New England.

One evening out son was having an asthma attack, His room was downstairs, just below our room. He didn't want us around when he was sick so I gave him a large bell and told him to ring it if he needed me.

When we went to bed, My husband Ray, fell asleep as soon as his head hit the pillow. I tried to fall asleep, but I could hear some talking. I listened very carefully to see if it was my son trying to call for me, or if it was the television. I looked outside the window to see if someone was in the church parking lot visiting. No one was there. As I strained to hear, a voice suddenly spoke to me. It was such a soft, wonderful voice—so beautiful. It said,

"If you would but trust me one more time, you could hear oh, so clearly."

I was not asleep and I knew I heard this voice and I responded to it out loud by saying "When did I ever trust you?" I knew this was not my Lord talking to me.

Now you have to know my background to understand my actions in what took place next. I came out of the church where you did not pray out loud. You bowed your head, closed your eyes and prayed to yourself. Only the Pastor prayed out loud. So when someone asked me to pray for them, I would always nudge my husband and ask him to pray. I was not comfortable praying out loud.

So when I heard this voice and recognized it as the enemy, I spoke out against it, in my mind. When I came against it, I heard another voice. It said "Rebuke him in the name of the Lord." I knew it was the Holy Spirit instructing me, so in my mind I started rebuking the enemy.

He (the enemy) said again in a whispery voice "Trust me." And again the Holy Spirit said "Rebuke him in the name of the Lord." Once again I started rebuking him in my mind. The Holy Spirit spoke again and said, "Rebuke him, <u>out loud</u>. He can't read your mind. He is the prince of the air."

When He said that, I knew it was true. So I tried to speak but I could not. I knew my husband was asleep, and I could not pray out loud. It seemed I struggled with the voices for several minutes.

They continued, "Trust me"...... "Rebuke him".... "Trust me"..... "Rebuke him"....

It was like the cartoon I've often seen of the devil on one shoulder and an angle on the other. Finally I said to myself, This is ridiculous I'm going to sleep" I flipped over on my side, tucked my hands under my cheek and tried to go to sleep.

The Holy spirit spoke one more time and said "Either you rebuke him right now, <u>out loud</u>, in the name of the Lord, or your son is his!"

The urgency of this statement rushed through my body. I could feel the blood draining from my face and myself turning white. I turned over and took a deep breath. I knew I had to do this.

So speaking only loud enough for my words to be put into the air I said, "Satan, you get out of here and leave my family alone. You get your hands off my son and my family and get out, in the name of Jesus, Amen."

What happened next blew me away. My husband still sound asleep said in a loud voice "Amen."

He never woke up. He knew nothing of what had just taken place. But "his spirit" dwelt with "my spirit" and the "Holy Spirit" for the soul of our son. This thrilled my soul, to think our spirits can come together in agreement, with the Holy Spirit.

I'd like to tell you that all was wonderful and miracles took place, but it didn't. A few days later I asked my son to leave home and he did. He went on with his way-word lifestyle for several years. He had some accidents where he damaged his back and he also developed Pancreatitis. He lived a life of much pain.

He had full and mischievous life. Thinking about how his dad was getting old, he wanted to come and live with us again, to be with his dad in his last years. Whether that was the real reason or not, we'll never know. But he couldn't work and by this time and was off illegal drugs, but was addicted to over the counter drugs. So we took our son back home and loved him, and enjoyed him most of the time. We could tell when he was being tormented by the enemy. When he was in pain he would always call 911. About three or four times a week we had an ambulance at our house. I don't know what the neighbors thought. We had only lived in the house about two months at that time. He had tried to get us to call 911, we refused. So he always had his cell phone at his fingertips. When we talked about the Lord, he would always say "I pray all the time. I love the Lord. It's the Christians I have a problem with."

In two thousand six my husband and I were both working with Teen Challenge in Florida. Our son was still living with us. He was home all day by himself and we felt bad about that, but we think it was just what the Lord had ordered. He had lots of time to deal with the issues of his life and talk to the Lord. We were there six months when we planned trip to visit our daughter Teri in Boston.

We left on a Wednesday morning to go to Clearwater to do some business for Teen Challenge and then we flew on to Boston. Our son stayed home.

On Thursday night, the first night at our daughter Teri's home, the Lord woke me at two o'clock in the morning, and said "I took Tim home."

I said okay, turned over and went right back to sleep. The next morning I woke up and I knew I'd had a Godly visit in the night. I rushed down stairs and asked my husband if he had tried Tim's phone. He said "yes, but no answer."

I had talked to Tim at noon on Wednesday and my husband talked to him about 6:00pm that night but we had not been able to get through after that. When Ray said he had not been able to contact our son, I told him to call the pastor and ask him to go by and check on Tim. If he, the pastor could not go, to call the police because something was wrong.

My husband called the pastor who said he was leaving the house then. He would go by the house, can call us. He did not call right away and when we tried to call him, his phone was turned off. I knew in my spirit Tim was gone. My husband kept saying, "Honey, you don't know that." I said "oh, yes I do." Then I told him about my visitor in the middle of the night. After 20 minutes the pastor finally called and said Tim had passed.

It was if I left my body and was standing in the corner of the room watching myself scream and cry. I wondered where all that noise was coming from. I had never cried like that before. I can't even tell you how my husband reacted. The time is a blur. The next day we flew back to Florida, but I have no memory of that. Unless you have lost a child, even one that's 43 years old, you have no idea about the pain the parents are going through. My husband and I are pastors and have been with many people when they have lost loved ones, but we really didn't know until that experience, just how they were hurting.

My mother lost an eleven month old baby when I was two years old. When I was thirty, I asked her one day "Mama, do you ever think of Kenneth?" Her answer shocked me. She said "A day never goes by that I don't think of him." At time I thought that was very strange and unbelievable. Now, I understand. A day never goes by that I don't think of Tim and ponder things gone by. Which brings me to the scripture of seeing through the glass darkly? You'll understand it better by and by.

1 Corinthians 13:12; For now we see through the glass, darkly; but then face to face: now I know in part; but then shall I know even as also I am known.

Because it was the weekend, we had to wait until Monday night before we could view the body. He died Thursday morning, and because he lay there over twenty four hours, his body had swollen. I didn't think it looked like him so I couldn't go too close or really say anything to him.

My husband and daughter went directly to his body and loved him and talked to him. But I stayed at his feet, holding them through the blanket.

We didn't know what to do; we were from Oklahoma and had only been in Florida six months. We felt so alone. We were in a new place and really had no family or friends. We worked all day and only knew the other counselors at work and the men in the Teen Challenge programs.

We called our family funeral home in Oklahoma. They were wonderful and so much help. They were Christians and attended the same church we had for thirty years. With their help, we took our sons body home, back to Oklahoma for the burial.

That is where and when the answers came! Remember earlier I told you about the pact that God made with me about my sons soul? If you are not in the habit of listening when God speaks, then you are missing out on a great blessing. I had the assurance that God would save our son. In fact, when our son was at his worst and 30 yrs. old, I used to pray "Lord save him and take him home" so that we didn't have to watch him live for the devil. Little did I know! Be careful what you say or pray for.

At the funeral our former-son-in-law Tony, told us he had a message for us, given to him that morning by the Holy Spirit.

Tony, (who holds the office of a prophet) was in the shower preparing for the funeral. The Holy Spirit spoke to him and said "I have a word for Ray and Barbara." Tony acknowledged His presence and he said all he could do was stand there with water running over him. He was in awe of what he was hearing. When he got out of the shower the Holy Spirit told him to write it down. He told the Holy Spirit he was going to be late, and he would write it down later. The Holy Spirit said to him "Ok be on time and disobedient." Tony stopped in his tracks got a pen and paper and wrote down what he had been told. That afternoon he brought it over to our grandson's house and gave it to us.

Prophecy

"I am the Lord God, and I am He that searches the hearts of man. Just as my laws of seed time and harvest are constant in the earth, So are my laws of life and death, for life it is incomplete without death to fulfill it. And life is swallowed up in death, but quickly breathes new life once again in something new. Unlike the waves of the ocean, that roll over the sand of the beaches, washing away any footprints of passers by, Death does not weaken life, but empowers it. I, the Lord of Host, declare this day that I Am the same God that you made your vows to many years ago, and I have fulfilled all that I said I would do.

Behold I am God, draw close unto me and my Word and I will surely birth a new thing in you, and Life will once again spring forth!"

Now when I read these lines, (underlined) I knew exactly what they meant. Tony thought it meant something else, but I said, No, I know without a doubt what He is saying to me." This was a reminder and conformation that God did take my son home, just as He said He would that late night in 1990. Satan did not get my son's soul.

Now the one thing that my husband had a hard time with, was that our son was alone when he died. It had bothered Ray for two years.

Everything that I'd had a hard time with, God had given me peace about through dreams or visions or just talking to me. My husband said "why can't I get some peace?" God is so good. All you have to do is ask and listen.

Matt. 7:7; Ask, and it shall be given you; seek, and ye shall find; knock, and it shall be opened unto you:

Ray was on his way to a board meeting at the church, and came in to kiss me bye. As he walked out of the room, the Holy Spirit said to me, "I had to take Tim at that time because if you (meaning Ray) were there, you would have brought him back. Those words brought peace to my husband. Just the thought that God cared enough to send him a message, built his faith greatly. I told him that there was another message also… "That he had the power to raise the dead" John 14:12.

You see God took our son while he was ready. God knows our future and He knew it was now or never. I would rather lose him now and know he made it to heaven that for him spend eternity in hell. In comparison, it was a small price to pay.

People often ask us what our son died of. We would always say a heart attack, but we really didn't know. They did not do an autopsy. They told us he just melted to the floor. That he was standing beside the bed, looking through his brief case and just melted to the floor. Now if he'd had a pain he would have called 911. His cell phone was within arms reach. So we just assumed he had a massive heart attack.

Sometime later, someone ask me what he had died from and I started to say he had a heart attack and God stopped me and said, "I told you, I took him home."

Well, I had read in the Word where He did this, but have never heard anyone nowadays, say such a thing. I didn't know God still just took people home, in that manner. Although the Word says the hairs on our heads are numbered; until now, I never gave it a thought. But now when people ask, "what did you son die of?" I always say "God just took him home". That's what God told me and I cannot lie.

Matt. 10:30; But the very hairs of your head are all numbered. Numbers 23:19; God is not a man, that he should lie; neither the son of man, that he should repent: hath he said, and shall he not do it? Or hath he spoken, and shall he not make it good?

"He's Alive, He's Alive"

The Prophecy was not the last confirmation I got from God. A few months later I was having a time with grief, thinking I did not tell Tim goodbye. God gave me a dream that night. In the dream we were ready for the funeral and I kept telling my husband, "I needed to tell him good bye." So he took me in where they had Tim laying, so I could say good bye. I walked over to him and looked down at him. He opened his eyes, looked up at me and smiled and said, "Hi, sweetie," That's what he called me. I screamed, "He's alive, He's alive. We can't bury him. He's alive."

My husband came to me and took me out of the room. I told him I needed to talk to Eileen, a friend of ours. About that time Eileen and her whole family walked out of the sanctuary. I said "Eileen I have to talk to you" She said "Barbara, I can't talk now, we've got to go."

Her daughter said "mom, you guys go on I'll stay here with Barbara." The hallway of this building was huge, at least 20 feet across. It had a large brown leather couch against the wall with beautiful pictures and plants everywhere. She took me to one of the couches, and sat me down. She said, "Now, what is it Barbara?"

I said "Lafonda, he's not dead. He's alive!" And at that moment the Holy Spirit spoke to me and said, "You're right. He is alive."

I woke up and again I knew I'd had a visit from God himself giving me peace that passeth all understanding. Peace that only God can give. I don't know why I'm so blessed. Or why God has chosen me to hear his voice. I went to scripture and I found "let he who has an ear hear." You can find this scripture several times in the Bible. Phil. 4:7: and the peace of God, which passeth all understanding, shall keep your hearts and minds through Christ Jesus.

Is God trying to talk to you? Do you listen to that still small voice? Have you ever started to do something, and then didn't? And you thought, oh, I knew I should have done that?

That was the Holy Spirit! He cares about the smallest things in our lives. That's how He trains us to hear His voice.

"Let he who has an ear, hear." (Matt. 11:15)

Our church, last year, decidied to write a book of Psalms, We called it the Psalms of Bethel. I woke up one night and started writing, and wrote four Psalms. One of them was about my son. It was called:

"A Guiding Force of the Holy Spirit"

Father, the Words that You have given me, have been kept as treasures. I long for more. We made a pact, so many years ago, and You kept your Word. Not only did you keep Your Word, You reminded me that you did. Even as You came to me in the middle of the night, to tell me of Your visit, and Your task, As sad as the message was, I had peace. Lord, your peace is so dominating and peaceful at the same time. You are awesome! I thank You Father, for the guidance that You send to me. In so many ways. Some from reading Your Word, and some by loved ones, through conversation, and some through prophecy and even the enemy himself. But when he talks, I know it's not true. For Your Word says "My sheep know My voice." It amazes me, every time the enemy comes to me, and I tell him to go away. And You speak, and my heart just opens wide. Thank You, Father. I've wasted so many years learning such simple lessons. And I have so much more to learn. But with Your help and guidance, I will become what you want me to become. Lord, I will set to memory the things You teach me. I will keep as treasures, the visits from Your Holy Spirit. I will bless Your people and win the lost for you. I wait patiently for Your training. Barbara Myers.

I have written many Psalms since that day. (I will add them to the back of the book for your pleasure.)

I love it when the Lord comes to me. It is a privilege that I can't explain. I have had many visions, and dream, and visitation from God. One was not too long ago.

Vision of the Dog

It was really strange. It was a vision. Again my husband was asleep and I lay there beside him on my side facing him. I opened my eyes and there sitting on him, was a very large dog. I closed my eyes and opened them again and it was still there. I raised my head up and it was still there. He had a very large head with a square jaw. There seemed to be light around his face that I could see his teeth and mouth very plainly. He was a large breed dog with brown and black colors. I later discovered, by checking dogs on the internet, it was a Rottweiler. He was just sitting there, his paws together, with his tongue hanging out, panting like dogs do. I knew it was something from God because there was total peace in the room and I was not fearful of the dog. I watched for a moment and the dog yawned. When he did this, a light came out of his mouth lighting up the whole room. Then the vision was gone. I pondered over this for the next three days, and finally the Holy Spirit told me the meaning. " The words that come out of our mouth should be the light of the Word. Tell what I want you to tell." That is another reason I am writing this book.

You see I've had many people tell me to tell this story, that it would help many other people. So I am trying to be obedient to God and the Holy Spirit.

May my words and experiences be one that will bless you and help you through many times.

A Dream from God

As He has done many times before, God came to me in a dream that has impacted my life. Since He has come to me before, I know when it's a Word from Him. At this time we lived in Florida where we both were counseling at Teen Challenge.

The Dream

I was walking on a slanted hillside lawn outside of a large building. There were lots of people walking around in that area. It felt like a college campus. Although I never went to college so why I felt that way, I don't know.

Someone pointed to the sky and said "what's that?"

I turned and looked up and what I saw took my breath away. It seemed to be one a platform of some kind, with an angel and three people on it. I couldn't see a platform, it just seemed like there had to be one. It was descending a a rapid pace, yet it didn't seem like it was moving fast at all. It just swooped down very graceful.

I knew immediately this was not any angel. He had an authority and majestic aura all around him. This angel stood tall with his shoulders back, and his wings flared higher than his head and they flowed downward touching the ground. The angel was at least seven feet tall, although the three people with him were very short, they looked just alike and had buster brown hair cuts. It was breath taking.

The other people on the lawn didn't seem surprised or excited to see such a phenomenon. I was in such a weakened state; I fell to my knees and started weeping and praying in the Spirit. I couldn't believe how loud I was crying. I couldn't even look up to see what was going on. I was in awe of his presence. When the angel landed on the lawn he gave a salutation of some kind. Something in the order of "Greeting from the MOST HIGH GOD" of "FROM ON HIGH."

I went completely limp. The message lasted for some time I think. I don't remember them leaving, I don't remember anything else until I was walking in this large building. I saw a lady (who was an old friend who was instrumental in my Christian background) and asked her directions for the restroom. She said it was down two steps.

I started down the steps and turned and said "did you hear what happened?" she replied "Well, I heard but I'm not sure I believe it." I turned and was leaning up against the door rail and said "Oh, honey, it's true, I was there." And I went weak again and started sliding down the wall weeping. I could feel the presence of the Lord all over again.

I woke up at that point and went to the bathroom. As I walked past the mirror I noticed my eyes were swollen almost shut from crying. I got back in bed and Ray said, "An angel touched my toes."

I thought he was talking about a real angel and that he had seen the angel too. I got excited and asked him if he saw the angel? But he was just talking about me. He said I touched his toes when I walked past the foot of the bed. I told him I didn't know I touched his toes. It was 3 A.M.

As I lay back down in my bed, I felt the presence of the Lord, it was so awesome, I love when he visits me. I knew it was a dream from God but I didn't know what it meant. I know the angel had brought a message but I didn't hear it.

I was weeping too loud and was in shock I guess. When I told Ray the dream I wept again. The presence of the Lord lingered for several days in my bedroom. Everytime I walked into my bedroom, I would get weak again and start crying. Now, I've pondered much about this dream trying to figure it out. I've prayed and asked God to reveal to me what the angel said. I wasn't happy with the answer, because it meant I would have to work for it. He said, "There was a message, but it was not for your flesh for your Spirit man."

That's why I couldn't hear him talking. And in time I will know what God dealt with me about. So I had to spend much time in prayer to get an interpretation or "my interpretation."

I praise Him with my whole heart and feel so humble for the privilege of His visits. You see about six weeks later we lost our son, so I thought maybe that's what the dream was about. Preparing me, for the loss of my son. But still I had to figure it out, with the help of the Holy Spirit.

I think the three people with him, was the senders of the message, The Father, Son, and the Holy Spirit. The building, I believe was a library, meaning I was to receive wisdom and learning of the new ministry God has for me.

The 2 steps I had to go down; one, the mourning of losing my son, the other a learning process of study and getting alone with God. I also think that whatever God has for me, the people will be slow to receive, because the friend in the library, that had a big part in my Christian life, even she didn't believe. Or maybe she will be the one to help me with the two steps. I don't know…

Since that time God has blessed me with a new ministry, new boldness, gifts of prophecy and interpretations, and an anointing of words that just flow from my mouth. Maybe they are the light of my Word, as in the vision of the Rottweiler. All I know is I have such a hunger for the Lord and His Word. I want everyone to have this hunger. I keep telling people to listen to the voice of the Holy Spirit. God said "My sheep know My Voice" If He wasn't going to talk to us, why would we need to know his voice.

God's Arrows of Love

This story happened years ago but taught me a big lesson.

It was probably the first lesson that God taught me. It was about 1977, give or take a year. I was visiting my sister in Missouri. Once a year I would go spend a week with her and her family. My sister and I have always been very close. While I was there I'd always do my Bible study. When I'd get my Bible and sit down, Betty's kids would all run up to me and sit around me. They loved my stories.

The last time I was there, Betty's husband came home and was standing at the door listening to me talk. I was talking about prayer. He was very interested in what I was saying, and was unusually tender so I turned my attention to him. I said something about him praying. He quickly withdrew and said "I don't know how to pray."

I tried to explain, and as if he realized we were talking religion, he changed back to a tough guy, and quickly said "Hey, I'm the meanest man in town, God don't want to talk to me," and with those words he left the room.

When I got back to Oklahoma and my normal routine, I couldn't get him off my mind. I wrote him a letter. I marked the envelope personal, so he would ne be embarrassed about us talking about God. You know how these tough guys are, they think only sissies talk about God and only sissies cry.

My sister told me she found the letter and that it would keep finding its way to the top of his pile of stuff. Which meant to me, he kept reading it. He never replied, and never answered the letter. In fact we never talked again.

About three months later he was killed in a one car accident.

After the accident he lay in a field all night. The next morning when they found him, he had a fist full of wheat in his hand. The doctors say he lived about six minutes after the accident.

At the funeral I was beside myself. He was my favorite brother-in-law. I was devastated because I didn't know if he ever talked to God. I stood there, pounding on the side of his casket crying "Why didn't you listen to me?"

Three months later I was in a church service, as a missionary was talking about the hunters in the area of Africa he was in. He mentioned how they had several arrow heads that they used for hunts. Different arrow head for different animals. He told us about the long narrow ones, the triangle ones, the scalloped ones, and the he said it. He talked about the jagged arrowhead that they used for the tough hided animals, which they called the tough kill. With this arrow they would shoot the animal and the arrow would just break the skin, but would not go in very far. Then as the animal walked away the arrowhead would work its way into the animal until it hit a vital spot. The hunters would track it until they had their kill.

At that point I zoomed out. It was as if the Holy Ghost told me to open my Bible and write down what he said. Now I had never done any writing before, so I was at a loss at what He was doing. I found a blank page in the back of my Bible and started writing.

God's Arrows of Love

Was I the arrow shot by God,
Into my loved one's heart?
Did I hit the target meant,
Or did I miss the spot?
Was I jagged from the start,
To work my way into his heart?
Was I the arrow shot by God
Into my loved one's heart?
Did God shoot me from His bow.
Did I waver to and fro,
Or did I hit the intended goal?
Was I the arrow shot by God
Into my loved one's heart?

It was as if my brother-in-law was the tough skinned person, he had to think a long time before he would make a decision. I didn't hear anything else the missionary had to say. I sat there wondering "well, was I?" I wondered and wondered, "Why didn't I get an answer? Four weeks later God gave me the ending to my poem. 'Yes, God did use me. Heart and soul, To win this loved one to His fold.

This was the only poem I had ever written at that time. God knew my heart. He knew I was hurting with no way to get an answer or to get any relief from my grief. The only clue we had that he may have talked to God was the fistful of wheat. Have you ever seen a picture of a circle and a fistful of wheat in it and above it was the word PEACE? He also gave me a scripture to go with this Word.

Ezekiel 33:7-8: God cares for me, and He cares for you. If you are hurting, He knows it. He felt your pain before you knew you were hurting.

When God tells you to do or say something, don't be afraid to step out and do it. It may be a one time thing. And it may just be what needs to be said at that time. It may win a soul to the Lord. And he may only ask you once, be ready.

"Let he who has an ear, hear" Matthew 11:15.

Boulders in Your Path

While sitting in church one Wednesday night, a young man was speaking and he kept saying "I talked to God for two hours and He said he would be here tonight. He is going to show up here tonight."

While he was still talking the Lord gave me a vision. The vision was of the Lord walking down a dusty road. All I could see was the bottom of His robe and His feet, but I knew it was the Lord. He walked down this road on His way to our church, (I presumed) and He came upon a large pile of basketball size boulders. He would not pass. Immediately some of us ran and removed our boulders.

How we knew that they were our boulders I don't know. We just did. Others in the congregation did not move. So those of us that had moved our boulders offered to remove the others and Jesus said, "NO. They have to do it themselves."

So I asked Jesus what does this mean and He said "These are controlling spirits that each person has and needs to get rid of." Then He took me to the 13 chapter of 1 Corinthians to the Love chapter. This tells us what He expects of us, but the things written on the boulders were jealousy, envy, haughtiness, selfishness and rudeness. Also the demanding our own way, irritability, touchiness, grudges, as well as self-centeredness, lazy, and controlling. He willnot come and tarry in the presence of these spirits. And yes, they are unloving spirits. In looking farther I found in Romans 1:29-30 almost this very same list.

Psalm 51:10: "Create in me a clean heart, O God; and renew a right spirit within me."

Our church has had several warnings from the Holy Spirit, but the enemy has our people blinded. Because they are all saints of the Lord, they can't believe that they are doing anything wrong. We need to examine ourselves daily, Luke 9:23. We have not arrived. We have a ways to go yet. It would be wise to ask the Lord every night if you have disappointed him today.

Now this vision has not faded away. Our pastor went out and bought 7 basketball sized boulders. He put signs on each listing the sin or spirit and where it is found in the Bible. The people responded positively. The next week our pastor went out and bought about 20 baseball sized rocks. It was communion Sunday, and he told the people to come get a rock, name it, and place it before the Lord, before taking communion. When the pastor called the people forward, they almost ran to the church altar, and the rocks were all used. The rocks are still at our altars today and are used frequently. God works in mysterious ways.

The Back Side of the Cross

The treasures of the heart cannot be hidden, but are manifest through words. In Mark 11:23 Jesus tells you that you can have what you say if what you say comes from faith in your heart. Learning to take the Words of Jesus personal, He wants to be personal with us. He walked and talked with Adam and Eve. He walked and talked with Abraham and Moses, and Elijah, and more. He wants to walk and talk with us too. Why isn't this happening?

You need to talk His language, hold no grudges, always forgive, and live love. "Whatsoever a man sows, that shall he also reap" We need to spend more quality time with our Lord and Savior. How many of you put God first in your life? Do you ever put Him on hold while you do something else?

When you get real hungry for a taste of the Lord, do you let other things distract you? Do you say, "I'll be back, Lord. Hold that thought?

You know you can never get that time with Him back. It's lost. Really, who is first in your life? I know you want to say God, but who really is? What takes you from His presence? What are your priorities? Do you really want revival? Are you afraid of the time or money that will be expected of you? That's flesh thinking… you have to think spiritual. If you deny yourself, you will hunger for God and Godly things…

You need to ask God to clear you thought process. You know the renewing of your mind.

Romans 12:2: "And be not conformed to the world; but be ye transformed be the renewing of your mind, that ye may prove what is that good, and acceptable, and perfect, will of God."

When we are hungry we plan three meals a day and even get a snack in between meals. Isn't out time with God, just as important? Shouldn't we plan our time, so that we include God in our daily activities?

I have had many special times with my Jesus… but I have a very special time that stand out in my mind. It was at a Tuesday morning prayer meeting. That particular week, we decided to ask God for nothing. Instead we just praised Him and thank Him and love Him for what he had done for us. I sat there on the floor and I praised and praised and I thanked Him until I was at a loss for words. Then I praised Him in a heavenly language. Finally I said "Lord, I thank you that I have shoe laces for my shoes. At that time I was humbled to the point that God poured out on me the most wonderful blessing. I was in his presence. I had nothing I could hold in my hand, but presence of the Lord was something I will take to heaven with me.

There are some things that are priceless. You see, it wasn't a ten minute prayer. I sat there for over forty five minutes of prayer and praising before I broke through. It was worth the wait! "For they that wait upon the Lord shall renew their strength." (Isaiah 41:31)

Another experience I'd like to tell you about is the day I found a personal relationship with Jesus. "Ask and ye shall receive"

In February of nineteen eighty one, I owned my own bakery. One Sunday morning at church, our church bus captain reported to the pastor that a man needed prayer. So our pastor sent my husband and another pastor to pray with him. Much to their surprise, when they got to the house, they found a Demon possessed man. I spent that afternoon decorating Valentine cookies. Four hours later when I got home, my husband was still not home. When Ray walked in the house and I could tell he had had an experience to behold.

They had just spent four hours praying with a Demon possessed man. We've heard about things like this, but had never come in contact with it before. They prayed and cast many spirits out of him. He responded in a vicious way. First, he tried to bow down to them and they told him to get up. They did not receive it. He tried to hit them and his fist would not go any closer than one foot from their face.

He pulled the phone out of the wall when they tried to call for help because they were becoming weary. He tried to throw things at them only to become very stiff and turn the other way before he threw it. He took his shirt off and flexed his muscles. They told him he was defeated two thousand years ago, and he ran to the kitchen and huddled in a corner in the fetus position. The man became tired and lay down on the couch and fell asleep. When he awoke, he tried to ask for help, but in the middle of the sentence his voice would change to an ugly gravely sound and he could not plea for help. He fell on top of the coffee table and the table danced around the room. He even slithered like a snake on the floor. Finally after many spirits left, the man prayed the sinner's prayer.

Now I've told you this, to tell you how and why the Holy Spirit spoke to me the next day. As I stood over the furnace the next morning my husband walked through the living room. The Holy Spirit spoke to me and said "You won't make it to Heaven on his shirt tail."

My testimony is not one of a big sinner. You see, I had always been a good person I didn't drink or smoke or do any off color things. I had a very strict father, and was always afraid to do something wrong. So when I gave my heart to the Lord, I didn't feel like I had given anything up in return for my salvation. I believed in God the Father and in Jesus the Son and the Holy Spirit, but I really didn't have a personal relationship with Him, so I was just living through my husband's relationship with Him, I didn't pray out loud, I did not even read out loud. If someone asked me to pray, I would nudge my husband and he would pray. I praised God that I was never without my husband. But the day came that God demanded something of me. I had to make a stand for myself.

So one afternoon I got my Bible and sat down in the living room floor and started praying. I would pray for a while and I would read the Word for a while. I'd pray in tongues. Then I'd cry and cry. An again and again this went on. It seemed like forever. Finally, I said, "Father, if I was in church and You had a message for me, there would be a message and interpretation and I would know it was for me. Will you do that?"

And I started praying in a tongue I had never spoken in before and when I finished, these words came out of me (much to my surprised) "My child you are mine. I love you. Take my hand and seek comfort in My Word." I was so moved, I cried and cried, prayed and prayed, and ask for more.

Now if anyone had come to my door at this time they probably would have called for help. I wasn't the quietest and it went on for about two hours. I kept asking for a personal relationship with Jesus. I just had to have something to hold on to. I knew I loved him, but who was this thing, this person, that I loved so dearly. I had to have an answer. Finally I said, "Father I want to see Jesus." Someway, somehow I needed to see Him. I just had to have a personal relationship with him.

Finally, I was taken to the backside of the cross. I can still close my eyes and see the back side of the cross. I could see His legs moving. They were bent and bleeding. There were people standing around. When the vision was over, I felt even worse, because I was not worthy to be taken to the front side of the cross. (What I didn't realize at the time was, I couldn't have stood seeing what He looked like from the front side).

Even though I got my personal touch with Jesus, I didn't understand it until nine months later when the pastor of a Connecticut church called and wanted us to come and tryout for a position in his church. When we walked into the foyer of that church, there hanging on the wall was the very vision He had given me nine months earlier. This painting was painted by a lady in their church and it was one of a kind. It was her rendition of the back side of the cross. God used this vision as a confirmation of our position in that church. He is so wonderful, why we doubt or worry about anything is beyond me. He has our life all mapped out, if we but give Him control.

Every chance I got I would stand before that picture and it showed me many things. The one that I remember the most about the painting is that in the rocky hill there was nothing but rocks and hard ground. This artist painted a strip of green grass and flowers. It was in, and only in the shadow of the cross. This showed me that there is "life in the shadow of the cross." He took me to the back side of the cross where there is life in His shadow. That painting was truly inspired by God.

Uncle John's Story

Some years ago, I had, what I thought was a strange dream. Yet, I somehow knew, that this was for a reason but did not know what it could be. In this dream my sisters and I, we were at a wake for my Uncle John. It was back in the times where the body laid in state at the home.

This house had a long living room with a screen door in the middle, leading out to a long narrow wooden front porch. To the left of the screen door is where Uncle John was lying. Just across from this screen door against the wall, was a couch. Three of my sisters and I were sitting on this couch, talking and laughing.

Our dad walked out of a bedroom and walked across the floor to a screen door. He walked out and walked all the way to the end of the old wooden porch.

Now Uncle John was lying on this bed in front of the window across the room from where we were sitting. All of the sudden, Uncle John sat right up in the bed. He turned and got off the bed and walked to the screen door. Daddy turned and looked at him and said, "What is it John?" Uncle John said "I just came back to let you know it's ok." And at that being said, Uncle John returned to his bed, lay down and was dead again.

You have to admit this was a strange dream. I never forgot the dream and thought of it often. But in that place of my life, I didn't think about asking God for the meaning of the dream. Then the day came when I got that phone call. My sister Donna called and said daddy had a heart attack. We lived four hours from my parents. I called my sister in Fargo, Oklahoma and told her to come quickly. We started toward Cushing, Oklahoma, where mama and daddy lived. It was raining so hard we had to pull over several times to wait on the rain to let up. I prayed and prayed. I prayed that God would send someone to daddy, because I knew he was not born again. I didn't want him to go to hell.

Oh yes, we had tried to talk to him about this but he would always say, "I'm ok, you just take care of yourself." He believed in that old saying that Christians are sissies. I think he believed in God, but had no idea he had to except Jesus as his savior.

As we traveled, I prayed several ways. I asked God to send someone to him, to pray with him. I asked to have a Christian nurse when we got there, if he was still alive. That's when I asked God to send Uncle John to him, just like in the dream and let him know it was okay to love the Lord. (Okay, meaning he was not a sissy.)

Well, we did get there and he was alive, but they had lost him at one point and brought him back. They only let two people go in for ten minutes, every hour. We went in and the nurse was in the room. We started praying for him but did not pray in tongues out loud. Then we heard this little voice praying. I opened my eyes and it was the nurse with her hand on daddy, praying. God had not only given us a Christian nurse, but a spirit filled Christian. Ray asked him if he wanted us to pray and he nodded yes. Every time Ray went into the room he would indicate he wanted him to pray again. Ray prayed the sinner's prayer with him. After that time my little daddy was the sweetest and most gentle daddy a girl could ever want. I believe God sent Uncle John to daddy while he was out, and that Uncle John told him that it was okay! Just like in the dream.

My dream of Uncle John's wake was several years before Uncle John died. But he did die before my dad did. I knew he was in heaven, because my Ray had prayed the sinner's prayer with him too.

It's kind of a funny story. Ray and I took mama and daddy to Weatherford, to the hospital to see Uncle John because he'd had a heart attack. They would only let one person in the room at a time. Aunt Pearl told Ray to go on in. while he was in the room the rest of us walked down to the nurse's station. While we were standing there the monitor in Uncle John's room went off. We all rushed back down to his room. He was sitting up in bed praying the sinner's prayer with Ray.

It really upset Aunt Pearl. She said "what's he trying to do, kill him?" Uncle John's doctor was a Christian and would give him scriptures when he went in for his appointments, so I felt like he was in good hands. I don't remember when Uncle John died or how long Aunt Pearl lived before she died. While she was in the hospital, again we took mama and daddy to see her.

They had called in the family from California and Nevada. There was about ten of us in her room and someone said, "Maybe some of us should go to the waiting room." So we all started out, and Aunt Pearl said, "Is Bob Here?" That was my nickname. I responded and she said she wanted to talk to me, so all the others left the room. I went over to her bed side and asked what she needed. Her answer, to this day is a mystery. She said "I just wanted to tell you, that I talked to God the other day, and I told Him if He could forgive an old mean lady like me and if He could use me, in any way I would like that."

Revelations 3:20: "Behold, I stand at the door, and knock; if any man hear my voice, and open the door, I will come into him, and will sup with him, and he with me."

I didn't know what to say and don't remember what I did say. Except, my heart leaped within me. You see, in her way, in her words, she prayed a sinner's prayer. And without a doubt, God answered her cry and said "Come on in". Now, I couldn't understand why she wanted to tlel me this wonderful news, out of all her family. And she had Christian children that did not know.

After thinking about it, I thoguth it might be because she go so upset with us when Ray prayed with Uncle John. But she just didn't know how to say anything. It was hard for people back then to talk about these things. That's why my daddy would say, "I'm okay." It was because he didn't know how to respond to that kind of talk. I was honored that Aunt Pearl wanted to let me know that it was all right with her soul.

Even my little sister, did not understand the things of God. We need to realize that even today everyone does not know things that we know. Forty five years ago, Linda was eighteen years old and had come to visit us. We were talking one evening as I was embroidering. She was looking through one of the kids Bible books. She started asking questions. And as I answered them and told her how Jesus was born to a virgin, in a stable, she made a comment that floored me. She said, "I thought Jesus only walked in clouds." She didn't know the story of Jesus and how he was born on Earth. I know she went to Sunday school, and how these things did not get through to her I don't know. We talked a long time that might and I told her, "I think Jesus is knocking on the door of your heart."

She said, "Oh, I hope he comes in." so again in her own words and in her way she prayed a sinner's prayer. Just like Aunt Pearl. You see, it's not a set prayer that you have to pray when you talk to Jesus. It's you! Just you in your own way. God knows us each as an individual, and He knows our hearts. Anyway Linda, Ray and I prayed and the next Sunday at church she went forward to give a public profession of her decision to follow Jesus and live for him.

I think that everyone who knows her will say that she honored her commitment to God, and she does to this day.

I have relatives that do not believe in God or Jesus or the Devil. I have family members that are beautiful Christians, and probably some who have never given it a thought. But one day, and that day is coming very soon, they will give it a thought. The Bible says that every knee will bow and every tongue will confess that Jesus Christ is Lord.

Not only is there a Heaven and Hell, there is a spiritual world out there too. I can tell you some hair raising stories about the spiritual world. One was when we were in Florida, and my sister called the church just after service. I answered the phone and she asked to talk to Ray, which was strange. After all she was my sister.

Now my sister and her family were not Christians. When I would tell them things we were confronted with, they didn't believe us. Well she started her conversation out with, "now you won't believe this, but it's true."

And proceeded to tell us what had been going on at her house. I call this...

"Permission to Haunt"

While we were Pastors a small church in Palm Harbor, Fl. We received a phone call just as the service was letting out. The caller (which was my sister from Oklahoma) said "I need to talk to Ray." Now this was very strange because my family never called to talk to Ray, so I stayed on the line to see what was going on. My sister said, "Ray what I'm going to tell you may sound strange but it's all true."

Then she preceded to tell us about a haunting that was going on in her house. She had a spirit tormenting her and her family. She said it started out just like a cat walking at the foot of her bed.

It went from there to cuddling up behind her while she was in bed, and even to the extreme of massaging her shoulders. She was afraid to tell anyone, afraid they would think she was crazy. This had gone on for some time now and she finally told her daughter Sherri. Sherri told her to take her Bible to bed with her. Eunice, my sister said she did. She put it beside her bed. The spirit went back to shaking the bottom half of the bed. It would not cross over the Bible.

One night she heard her husband screaming "who in the *#** is trying to pull me outta bed?" My sister's husband was blind and had sugar diabetes, and was pretty much bed ridden. They slept in separate bedrooms. When he needed her he would call and she would come and take him to the bathroom, with the help of his walker. This one night she took him to the bathroom and lay down on her bed, waiting for him to finish and she fell asleep. While she slept, the spirit that had been tormenting her, used her voice, came and took her husband back to bed. In the process asked Otis, if it could stay there with him. Otis, thinking it was Eunice his wife, told him… "Yes, that's a stupid question, of course you can stay," thus giving the spirit permission to stay with them.

After it started tormenting Otis, Eunice and Sherri decided they had to do something about this. So they told Sherri's family, only to find out that her two teenage boys had been entertaining the spirit in their room. After the phone call to my Ray and after he heard their story, he prayed with both my sister and her daughter. They both turned their lives over to Jesus. My husband called two preachers he knew in Shattuck, Oklahoma. He asked them if they would go over and clean house for us. They said they would, and that is how we found out that the spirit had permission to stay. When they demanded that the spirit leave, it spoke to them and said, "I have permission to stay."

Plan B…. We had to go through Otis to get this job done. Sherri explained it all to her dad and called us again. My husband prayed the sinner's prayer with him but not without conflict.

In his younger years, Otis was a stutterer. He was now in his 70's and hadn't stuttered in years, but when Ray asked him to repeat the prayer he could not talk. Ray had to repeat it two and then three times before he could repeat the prayer. The spirit left but would come back periodically to torment my sister. This was fifteen years ago and even though they have moved to Missouri and Otis has passed away, the spirit still comes back to torment my sister to this day.

We are living in a spiritual battle field. We need to study our bible and find out what kind of weapons we are coming against. What we need to do to be prepared for such a battle. The Word tells us to put on the whole armor of God. What do we need armor for if we are not in a battle? Don't just read words when you read your Bible, read the meaning of those words. Ask questions, talk it over with family, It will bring your family closer together.

Face to Face with Demons

On about the 1st of April 2007, Ray and I went to New England to visit our daughter Teri. We also visited some good friends while we were there. We stayed a friend's home a couple of nights and then I went over to a girlfriend's house to spend one night. We had done this many times, and they had visited us in both Florida and Oklahoma. But this time I had an experience I will never forget. I was bringing her up to date on all I had been through the previous year. We had lost our son in December and I had been diagnosed with sugar diabetes. I was telling her how I overcame and why we moved back to Oklahoma. She was acting different. She herself had gone through a lot that year. She was overly affectionate, which wasn't too strange for her, for she is a very loving person, and she loves me like a sister.

But I was becoming very uncomfortable. I detected some strange feelings in the house itself. I overlooked it all evening, but when it came time to go to bed I was disturbed. She insisted that I sleep in her bed and she on the couch. I didn't want to do that since she had been sick, but I finally gave in.

She has a cat that will not let anyone see it. It would run and hide if someone came in the house. No one has seen this cat. While I was there the cat came out and sat at my feet, never hid or ran away. Strange!

Then while we were talking about my year, I was more or less preaching on the spoken Word and how you could speak to your body and be healed. She interrupted me in the middle of our talk and said "Oh, I want to show you something." She left the room and came back with one of those small desk calendars with jokes on each day of the year. She read about fifteen of them. I sat there in shock, since she interrupted me in the middle of such a serious conversation, for a joke. Especially since she and both her children have a death sentence illness.

Then she never went back to our conversation. Now it's not that she doesn't like to hear me talk, because she loves to listen to me when I teach or talk about the Lord. Now I could tell she did not realize what she was doing. It just wasn't her. We didn't have too much to talk about so we decided to go to bed.

She came in the room several times, to see if I needed anything. She turned the covers back for me. Then she said "Do you need anything?" I said no and she left the room. But in just a few minutes she came back and asked again "Do you want anything?" I said no and she left the room again, only to return a third time to ask if I needed anything. I felt she was not herself and seemed to be very distant. Again I told her no! She asked if I wanted her to shut the door. Well, the door could not close because of all the clothes that were hanging on it. So I told her just pull it to. And still again, she came back to see if I wanted anything. I was really feeling funny by this time. I had stayed at her home many times before and had never gone through this kind of stuff. I was starting to worry about her and her state of mind. I turned on the TV for a few minutes and then cuddled down to go to sleep.

In about 15 minutes, I was not fully asleep yet, but was far enough into a sleep that I had a dream of sorts. From the foot of the bed, a spirit crawled up on top of me, about up to my chest. I put my hands on top of its head and was screaming for my friend to come help me. I finally yelled loud enough to wake myself up. This spirit had a full head of hair. I knew this was an attack from the devil.

I took a couple of deep breaths and went back to sleep. Again in about 15 minutes another spirit crawled from the foot of the bed, only this time he was on the side of me. He came as far as my armpits and I put my hand on him and started screaming again. This demon was half bald and half hairy. He looked up at me and said "STOP." Again my screaming woke me up. This time I was getting a little scared of the activity. I turned the TV back on and flipped channels for a while. My nose started running fiercely, so I got up and took a sinus pill. My friend was asleep on the couch.

I lay back down turned off the TV and started to go to sleep. Within seconds a third spirit appeared in the doorway and walked over to the side of the bed. This time I was awake. He stood so close to the side of the bed that his form overlapped onto my arm. I felt a spirit of fear coming upon me. I remembered something I read in a book and I sat up in bed and said "In the name of Jesus get out of here right now and leave me alone, in the name of Jesus." I felt, and could almost see the spirit walk to the end of the bed and turn to go the corner of the room. I said, "I said get out, get out of that corner and leave now and don't came back, in the name of Jesus."

The hair on my arms and neck lay back down and I was at peace. I went to sleep and slept the rest of the night. Now this experience shook me a little since the Lord had been leading me into a deliverance ministry. I thought "wow! If I got scared, how can I be in deliverance ministry?" I couldn't wait to get home to ask Tony what the meaning of all this was.

This all took place about 2 A.M. I wanted to call my husband so bad but I knew if I did he would want to come and get me right away. And I didn't want to wake up everyone at Ken's house. My fear was that my friend was having some demon activity going on in her house and she didn't know it. I waited about a month before I ask her a question about what happened. She didn't know of anything wrong.

You know we are in a spiritual battle and warfare goes on all the time. If we but open the door a little, the devil will come in and devour. The Bible says, "He goes about like a roaring lion, seeking who he may devour." You don't find many who will talk about demons or evil spirits, but they are out there.

Angels in Boston

Not only is there a spiritual world out there, there are also angelic beings. While we were on staff in Boston when the Lord opened my spiritual eyes. We were sitting in service one morning and I saw three angels. They were all around the pastor. There were two very tall angels, one on each side of him and one small angel hovering over his head, pouring oil over him as he preached.

I didn't believe what I was seeing. In fact, I argued with myself that I was not seeing the angels at all. I thought I did, but I just couldn't have. I battled within myself for two days. I wanted to tell the pastor what I saw, but I couldn't believe I saw it. Tuesday mornings we had our staff meeting. I sat through that meeting in torture. I wanted to tell, but was afraid I would be lying. Just as they were starting to dismiss, I blurted out, "Pastor, I have to tell you something." I told him what I thought I saw and the associate Pastor spoke up and said, "You're the fourth person that has told us that very same story, word for word."

God opened my spiritual eyes that day and I almost let the enemy cheat me out of it. God blessed me that day with a gift of seeing through spiritual eyes. The Holy

Spirit is always trying to teach us lessons, but we often don't listen. Like I've said before, "My sheep know My voice." Why would we need to know His voice if He wasn't going to talk to us? "My people perish from lack of knowledge" Hosea 4:6.

The Holy Spirit seems to come to me at night or in the early morning. I guess that's when I'm most acceptable to His voice. It may be a different time for you. Watch for it! I'm believing after you read my book that you will start teaching yourself to listen for His voice, because He is talking to you.

One time I was trying to learn how to transfer pictures from my file into the church bulletin. I had asked two different people to come in and show me how to do it. They never had the time. I woke up one morning and the first thing on my mind was, go hit this button, and then this button and then that one. I jumped out of bed and ran to the computer and did just what I was told. It worked. I was so excited. I thanked the Holy Spirit for loving me so, and teaching me to listen when He talks. I wrote a sermon once called "Dare to Listen when God wants to speak". I wrote this book to help other who have gone through or are going through what I have. Being able to hear God's voice or learning to listen is all part of the process.

He speaks to us through His Word also. For instances the parables. Get your Bible and read the parable of the Ten Virgins. Study it, how does it fall into today's world and our life. What is oil? Where does it come from? Where do we put it, we don't carry lamps? You see you are listening with ears of flesh and not ears of the spirit.

For we are the lamps, the oil is the Holy Spirit, we put the oil or the Holy Spirit in our hearts and minds. When we were born again, we became as new babes in Christ. Listening, learning and living the Word of God. When we were reborn, He filled us with oil, (the Holy Spirit). As we use up that oil we are to refill ourselves with His Word and faith. Faith come from hearing and or reading God's Word. We think we are where we are supposed to be. But are we? Sunday comes around and we get up and go to church. Why do we do that? Is it a habit or do we have a burning desire to hear from God? Do we want to get together with other believers and give God the praise He deserves and wants? Did you get that? He wants our praise. He waits for it. But we come and sit in our chosen seat (provided no one else is sitting in it) and for some unexplainable reason we melt to that chair and don't want to move. It's a chore to stand to our feet or raise our hands or even utter a word out loud. We cant't even give Him our sacrificial praise. Why is this? Are we afraid that the person next to us will hear us praise the Lord? We should be jumping up and down, if only on the inside. If we are jumping up and down on the inside then it will show on the outside.

I was at a district meeting last night and a lady across the aisle was praising the Lord so openly I was blessed. I know God was receiving it all. After the service I went to this lady and hugged her and blessed her and I told her I was blessed by her uninhibited praise for my Jesus. Truly her lamp was full. My prayer is that when people see me, they see my Jesus in me.

When the trumpet sounds, there is no time to refill. When five of the virgins knocked on that door and said, "Lord, Lord open up for us, we are loyal servants." The Lord said, "Verily, verily, I say unto you, I know ye not." They waited too long to make sure your vessel was adequately filled.

Say you need a kettle of water, you would turn on the fire until it's hot. If you want it to stay hot, you would leave the fire burning, but if you don't think you'll need it until night time, you might turn the burner off. Therefore, the water gets cold, or at best lukewarm. Do we heat up the kettle on Sundays and set it on the back burner the rest of the week. Are you a wise virgin or are you a foolish virgin? Think about it! I need to make every effort to obtain every word God sends my way. Every service I go to is a banquet at the Lord's table. At this time I eat too much and get fat on His Word. May your time at the banqueting table be as fulfilling.

On the following pages are the Psalms that God gave me when we were making our book of Psalms for our church…

The Psalms of Barbara

A Touch of the Masters Hand

Oh, the wonder of watching You work.
To see You take a piece of clay
And mold it into a beautiful piece of art.
To watch You, oh Lord,
To see the wonder of You,
When You burn off the edges of the vessel.
To put it in the fire of Your Love
And to see You break off the dark
Places of the molded piece of art.
To see the colors come off Your brush,
And the new beauty burst forth
Into the "Son" light.
Oh Lord, just to be an instrument of You, that You might
　　use me to bring forth this piece of your art.
Thank you Father, that I too
Was once a piece of clay in your hands.

Barbara Myers

The Wondering Mind

Father, I go through my days whispering your name,
And talking to you, but at times, I don't feel your presence.
Are you there, even then?
Do you know what I am going through?
Do you really love me like they say?
Father, I know all these answers,
Why do they keep hounding me so?
I know You, or your love will never leave me,
That You are always there.
Always smiling at my doubts,
And at my lack of faith. And I know
You walk with me and talk with me,
I hear Your voice, and then, I don't hear it.
Why are things so confusing?
What is it that makes us talk to ourselves
And doubt our purpose in life?
Why are we always looking for more?
And always in the wrong places.
The peace I find, when I'm with You,
Is all satisfying, why look for more?
You said You made us in Your image,
Surely this is not like You, or is it?
You long for our praise,
Do You ever get enough?
Can Your Holy Spirit really hold us all,
As tight as we need to be held,
This one Spirit of You!
How can this be?
I know, but I don't know.
Father, sometimes my mind just
Floats around, thinking, is this wrong?

Barbara Myers

Silent Meditation

Father, how blessed I am.
I know You are no respecter of persons,
But at times, I feel like I'm Your favorite.
You have blessed me so much for so long.
Even before I gave my life and heart to You,
It seemed You had favor for me.
I go back years and years and can see times
When You placed Your hand over me for protection.
I know it was You, for no other would have cared.
I can shut my eyes, and paint a picture of
Angels, hovering around me as a child.
Even as a teenager they were there.
Lord, the life's mate, You chose for me,
Has served You well. Thank You Father, For a life of peace,
And even, me being a little naïve at times.
You have given me a protection from this world,
And even I don't understand why.
Is there a work, You have for me?
Am I where I should be?
I ask that question, knowing very well that I am not.
My laziness is a disappointment to You, I know.
And I'm sorry, as I say so often.
My spirit is willing but my flesh is weak.
But, that is no excuse. I'm guilty.
Lord, may I be a better daughter for You,
And for Your service.
May I spend more time in Your Word,
And on my knees,
And lying across my bed in silent Meditation....
This is one thing I have to do,
If only for my daughter..
My heart aches for my loved ones.

Barbara Myers

Use Me

Oh Lord, hear my prayer,
Lead me in the way You'd have me gg.
Father, birth in me, a new work.
Train me, break me, move in me.
Lord break my spirit
To be what I'm meant to be.
Let not my flesh control,
Father, have Your way in me.
Speak to me Holy Spirit,
Let Your voice ring in my ears.
Open my ears Lord, that I might hear,
That my spirit dwells with and in You.

Barbara Myers

How Deep, How Shallow!

Oh Father, How honored I feel,
To sit here night after night
And listen to a man without a voice box
Praise and worship You.
When those of us who have a voice, sit silent.
Oh Father, set our spirits free
That we might worship Thee.
Open our eyes Lord,
That we might see the things of You.
Oh, to be set free to worship
To worship openly, to be a witness to
And for You Father.
Oh Father, let us use this time to examine ourselves,
To see just how deep we are
Or how shallow.
Oh Father, search me, search my soul,
My heart, my mind, let me reveal to myself
Who I am and who You are.

Barbara Myers

Down in the Valley

Oh Lord, my heart is so heavy,
And I'm feeling so low,
And I know it's the enemy that torments me so.
I cry our to You Lord, for I know You are there.
I search my heart Lord,
For a reasonable doubt,
But for the life of me Father, I cannot see out.
It's the blinders I know,
That hinders my sight,
And keeps me awake, till the morning's light.
The tears I shed, only feed my woe.
Tell me, dear Jesus, where can I go?
I ask the questions and the answers I know,
For my Father in heaven is waiting for me,
To grab hold of the Comforter
He has sent "to me"

Barbara Myers

A New Day, A New Touch

Father, I'm standing on Your Word,
That Your angels will watch over us and all that is ours.
Lord, my heart is heavy tonight.
The memory of his arms around me,
And of his sister's remorse.
I feel so blessed that You have given me peace,
I know he is with You,
But the enemy keeps coming against me.
I'm so tired of fighting him off Lord,
I need new strength.
Strength that only You can give.
Father, I could use a visit.
You are so faithful,
So wonderfully patient with me.
When I need a new touch,
You give it to me.
Thank You Father

Barbara Myers

In Your Presence

Father, I watched as my sisters and brothers
Were submissive to your Spirit.
How Awesome!
Just to be in Your presence and watch You work.
You must have been pleased with Your children.
Father, the plans You have
For this small group of Saints,
Must be a heavenly assignment,
For the enemy keeps attacking.
But as we stand on Your Word
And claim Your promises, we will be victorious.
For since You are for us,
Who can be against us,
For "Greater is He that is in us,
Than he that is in the world."
We live in Your Words, Father.

Barbara Myers

A Cry of the Heart

Oh, Father, how I long for Your touch, For the sound of
    Your voice.
It's been too long since I sat still and listened,
For You to speak to me.
Father, I pray You will help me to be still
And wait patiently for Your Presence.
My memories are holding me for now,
But I long for a new touch, a new dream,
A new fragrance for Your presence.
Lord, I lay across my bed in anticipation of You.
I stand in a line, waiting for service,
And whisper Your name to myself.
How peaceful, even Your name is.
Thank You, Father,
For just the little things that keep me going.
I wait for the opportunity for You to use me.
I ponder, is this the time?
What do You want me to do?
Oh Lord, help me to be ready when the time comes
That I might be used of You.
Lord, let ne not be proud
But humble in Your presence, to do Your will.
Let my love for You show forth to others,
So they will know that You are not dead, but alive.
Alive in me, alive in them,
And in the world.

Barbara Myers

Slain

Lord, I saw You move last night
In a marvelous way.
When You touched me,
My whole insides lifted out of my body.
As I went to the floor, it was as if
I was a leaf falling from a tree.
I lay there in such peace, and
Didn't want to move,
Afraid I would lose the majestic feeling of Your presence.
What a sweet glimpse of heaven.
The work You did was all conclusive,
Even things I did not ask for.
You are so awesome.
Father, Your presence was so wonderfully felt.
Even the flesh in me had to yield
To Your heavenly presence.
Father, I yield myself to you.
My heart, my mind, my soul,
And my reason for being.

Barbara Myers

www.ingramcontent.com/pod-product-compliance
Lightning Source LLC
Chambersburg PA
CBHW071632040426